롤러코스터
이래서 강력추천합니다!

체계적인 학습 | 초등학교 교육 과정을 충실히 반영하고 교과서 지문을 최대한 활용함으로써 학생들이 배워야 할 주요 학습 내용을 체계적으로 익힐 수 있도록 하였습니다.

학년별 맞춤 학습 | 모든 학년에서 표현과 낱말 학습을 기본으로 하되, 1·2학년은 Phonics, 3·4학년은 Reading & Writing, 5·6학년은 Grammar를 다루는 등, 각 학년별 주요 학습 영역을 중점적으로 다룸으로써 학년별 맞춤 학습을 추구하였습니다.

균형적인 학습 | 읽기, 쓰기 학습뿐만 아니라 오디오 CD와 동영상 CD를 활용한 듣기, 말하기 학습을 통해 영어의 4개 영역(Listening, Speaking, Reading, Writing)을 고루 마스터할 수 있도록 하였습니다.

자발적인 학습 | Song, Chant를 통해 표현을 자연스럽게 익히고, Cartoon을 통해 배운 내용을 재미있게 정리하는 등 다양한 Activity를 통해 학생들이 흥미를 가지고 적극적으로 수업에 참여할 수 있도록 하였습니다.

동영상을 통한 원어민과의 학습 | 원어민의 발음과 입모양을 동영상 CD를 통해 정확히 인지하고 학습자의 발음을 녹음해 원어민의 발음과 비교하여 들어 보게 함으로써 학습자 스스로 발음을 교정할 수 있는 기회를 제공하였습니다.

01 Student Book

Conversation

초등영어 교과과정과 연계된 표현을
학습하고, 말하기 연습을 해본 다음,
다양한 확인 활동을 해봐요.

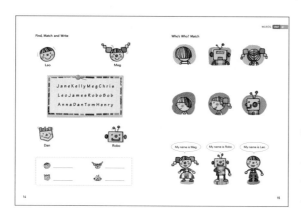

Words

생활 영어 표현과 관련된 낱말을 학습하고,
듣기, 읽기, 쓰기의 통합 활동을 통해
각 낱말을 익혀 봐요.

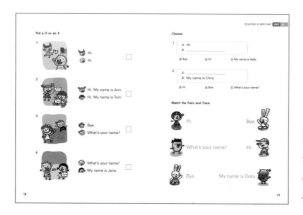

Reading & Writing

학습한 표현을 읽고 써 보면서, 표현에 대한
이해력을 높이고 자유롭게 활용할 수 있는
능력을 키워 봐요.

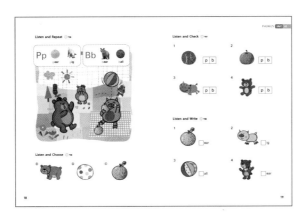

Phonics

목표 음가와 그 음가를 가지고 있는
낱말을 익히고, 다양한 활동을 통해
확인해 봐요.

Cartoon

재미있는 만화를 통해 이미 학습한
표현과 낱말을 종합 정리해 봐요.

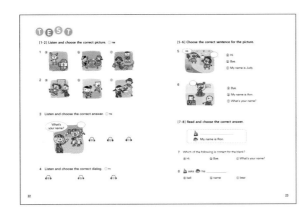

Test

테스트를 통해 학습한 표현 및 낱말에
대한 학습 성취도를 점검해 봐요.

02 Workbook

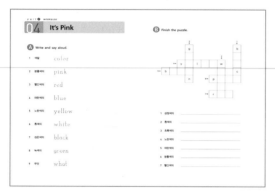

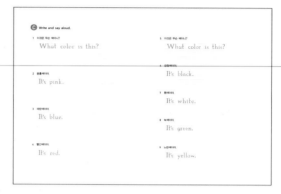

낱말을 따라 쓴 다음, 우리말에 해당하는 낱말을
직접 써 봐요.

표현을 따라 쓴 다음, 우리말에 해당하는 표현을
직접 써 봐요.

03 오디오 CD

Student Book의 내용과 노래 및 챈트가 담겨
있어요.

04 권말 테스트

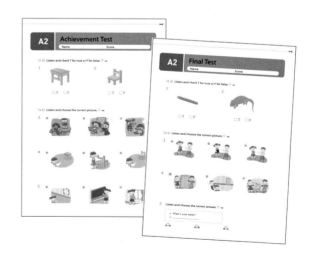

낱말 및 표현에 관한 문제를 풀면서 그동안 쌓은
실력을 마음껏 발휘해 봐요.
(Achievement Test / Final Test)

05 동영상 CD

Conversation

초등영어 교과과정과 연계된 표현을 배워 봐요.

Words

생활영어 표현과 관련된 낱말을 배워 봐요.

Phonics

목표 음가와 그 음가를 가지고 있는 낱말을
익혀 봐요.

Speak

원어민의 발음과 입모양을 인지한 후,
직접 녹음해 봐요.

Song & Chant

즐겁게 노래하고 챈트하면서 학습한 내용을
정리해 봐요.

Game

주요 낱말을 활용한 게임을 하면서 학습한
내용을 종합 정리해 봐요.

Learning Points

A1

Unit Title	Topic	Vocabulary
① Learning Aa~Ff	· Aa, Bb, Cc, Dd, Ee, Ff	apple, ant, arrow, boy, bee, ball, cap, car, cook, dog, dad, door, elbow, egg, elephant, flag, fish, fan
② Learning Gg~Ll	· Gg, Hh, Ii, Jj, Kk, Ll	girl, goat, guitar, house, hand, hat, iguana, insect, igloo, jacket, jeans, juice, kitten, king, key, leaf, lily, lion
③ Learning Mm~Ss	· Mm, Nn, Oo, Pp, Qq, Rr, Ss	mouse, milk, moon, nest, nose, nurse, ostrich, orange, octopus, pig, piano, pear, question, queen, quilt, rabbit, robot, rose, sun, socks, shoes
④ Learning Tt~Zz	· Tt, Uu , Vv, Ww, Xx, Yy, Zz	tiger, table, tent, up, umbrella, ugly, vest, violin, van, wolf, witch, web, fox, ox, box, yawn, yo-yo, yacht, zebra, zipper, zoo

A2

Unit Title	Function	Conversation	Phonics
❶ My Name Is Leo	· Greeting · Asking and giving names	Hi. My name is Meg. What's your name? My name is Leo. Bye.	First sounds P and B
❷ This Is a Chair	· Identifying objects in classroom	That is a desk. This is a chair.	First sounds T and D
❸ What's This?	· Identifying school supplies	What's this(that)? It's a bag(book).	First sounds K and G
❹ It's Pink	· Identifying colors	What color is this? It's pink. It's yellow.	First sounds F and V

A3

Unit Title	Function	Conversation	Phonics
❶ She Is My Mother	· Identifying family members	Who is he(she)? He(She) is my father (mother).	First sounds S and Z
❷ Are You Happy?	· Asking and telling about feelings	Are you happy? Yes, I am. No, I'm not.	First sounds H and J
❸ It's Sunny	· Asking about and describing the weather	How's the weather? It's sunny.	First sounds M and N
❹ Put On Your Gloves	· Commands	It's cold. Put on your gloves. OK, Mom.	First sounds L and R

Basic Commands

Roller Coaster
Contents

Listen and Repeat T02

Speak Aloud T03

 What's your name?

 My name is Tom .

1

Tom

2

Anna

3

Jenny

4

Your Turn

Listen and Choose T04

Kevin

 ⓐ   ⓑ   ⓒ

Find, Match and Write

Leo

Meg

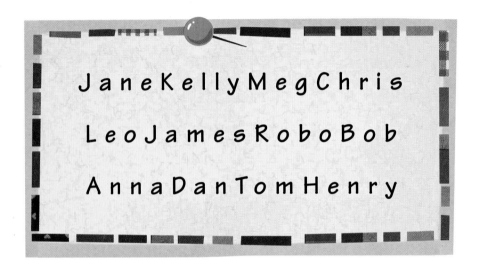

JaneKellyMegChris

LeoJamesRoboBob

AnnaDanTomHenry

Dan

Robo

Who's Who? Match

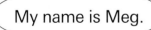
My name is Meg.

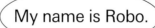
My name is Robo.

My name is Leo.

Put a O or an X

1

🙂 Hi.

😃 Hi.

☐

2

😄 Hi. My name is Ann.

😄 Hi. My name is Tom.

☐

3

😊 Bye.

😁 What's your name?

☐

4

😄 What's your name?

😊 My name is Jane.

☐

Choose

1

> *A:* Hi.
>
> *B:* _____

ⓐ Bye. ⓑ Hi. ⓒ My name is Kelly.

2

> *A:* _____
>
> *B:* My name is Chris.

ⓐ Hi. ⓑ Bye. ⓒ What's your name?

Match the Pairs and Trace

 Hi.

Bye.

 What's your name?

Hi.

 Bye.

My name is Dora.

Listen and Repeat 🔘 T05

Pp **pear** **pig**

Bb **bear** **ball**

Listen and Choose 🔘 T06

ⓐ

ⓑ

ⓒ

18

Listen and Check T07

1

 | p | b |

2

 | p | b |

3

 | p | b |

4

 | p | b |

Listen and Write T08

1

 ☐ ear

2

 ☐ ig

3

 ☐ all

4

 ☐ ear

Nice to Meet You

Read and Number

① name   ② Hi.   ③ What's your name?

TEST

[1-2] Listen and choose the correct picture. T09

1   ⓐ   ⓑ    ⓒ

2   ⓐ   ⓑ    ⓒ

3   **Listen and choose the correct answer.** T10

What's your name?

Meg

ⓐ   ⓑ   ⓒ

4   **Listen and choose the correct dialog.** T11

ⓐ   ⓑ   ⓒ

[5-6] Choose the correct sentence for the picture.

5

    ⓐ Hi.

    ⓑ Bye.

    ⓒ My name is Judy.

6

    ⓐ Bye.

    ⓑ My name is Ann.

    ⓒ What's your name?

[7-8] Read and choose the correct answer.

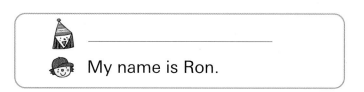

My name is Ron.

7 Which of the following is correct for the blank?

    ⓐ Hi.   ⓑ Bye.   ⓒ What's your name?

8 🔺 asks 🟤 his _____.

    ⓐ ball   ⓑ name   ⓒ bear

Listen and Repeat 🔘 T12

 **Let's Chant**

That is a chair.
No! No! That is a desk.
This is a chair.
I know. I know. This is a chair.

Speak Aloud T13

 This is a chair . That is a desk .

1 chair

2 blackboard

1 desk

2 door

Listen and Choose T14

1

2

Listen and Repeat T15

| blackboard | chair | desk | door | wall | window |

Listen and Choose T16

ⓐ

ⓑ

ⓒ

26

Look and Circle

1 　　door
　　　　　　　chair

2 　　desk
　　　　　　　window

3 　　wall
　　　　　　　desk

4 　　door
　　　　　　　wall

Find the Way

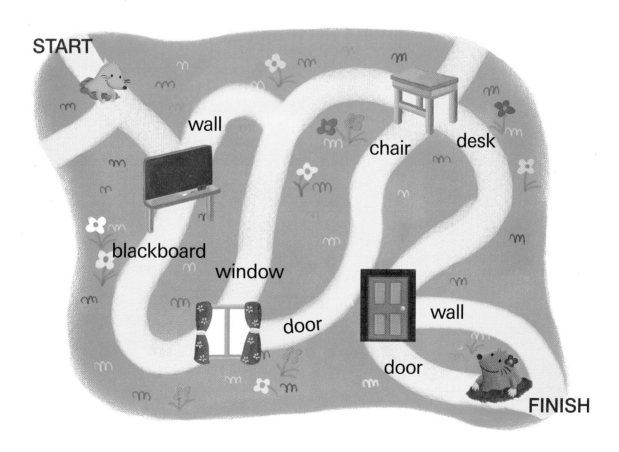

START

wall

chair　desk

blackboard

window

door

wall

door

FINISH

Read and Match

1

This is a chair. •

•

2

That is a window. •

•

3

This is a wall. •

•

4

That is a blackboard. •

•

Match, Write and Trace

1

2

3

_____ is a _____.

_____ is a _____.

_____ is a _____.

Listen and Repeat T17

Tt	top	tea	Dd	dog	doll

Listen and Put an X T18

ⓐ   ⓑ   ⓒ

Listen and Circle T19

1

t	d

2

t	d

Listen, Write and Match T20

1 ☐ea   2 ☐oll   3 ☐op   4 ☐og

Good boy, Pete!

Read and Number

① desk ② chair
③ This is a wall. ④ This is a door.

[1-4] Listen and write the number. 🔘 T21

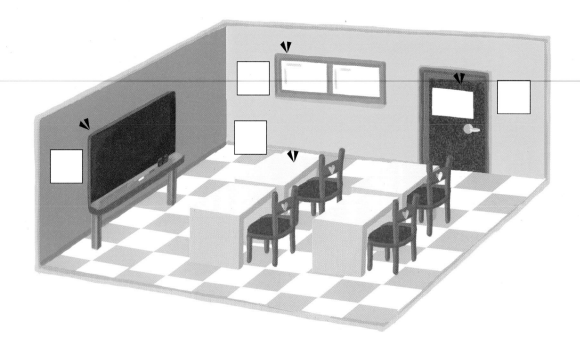

[5-8] Match the picture with the word.

5

6

chair　　wall

window　　door

7

8

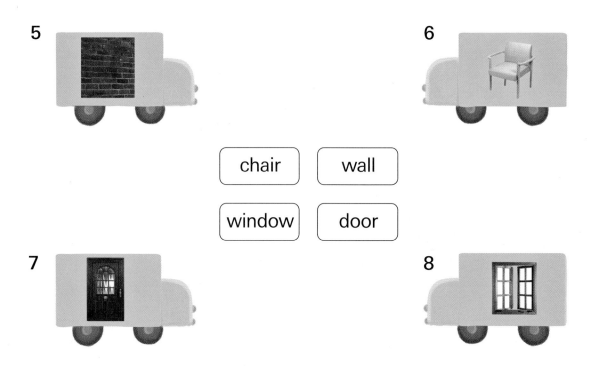

34

[9-11] Listen and choose the right picture. T22

9 ⓐ  ⓑ

10 ⓐ  ⓑ

11 ⓐ ⓑ

[12-14] Read and write the number.

12 _____ That is a wall.

13 _____ This is a chair.

14 _____ That is a blackboard.

UNIT 03 What's This?

What's this?

It's a bag.

What's that?

It's a book.

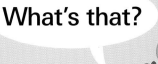

Let's Chant

What's this? What's this?
It's a bag. It's a bag.
What's that? What's that?
It's a book. It's a book.

36

Speak Aloud T24

1

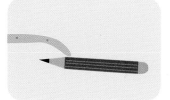

this / pencil

2

that / book

3

this / ruler

4

that / bag

Listen and Choose T25

Listen and Repeat T26

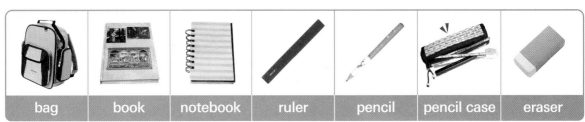

| bag | book | notebook | ruler | pencil | pencil case | eraser |

Listen and Number T27

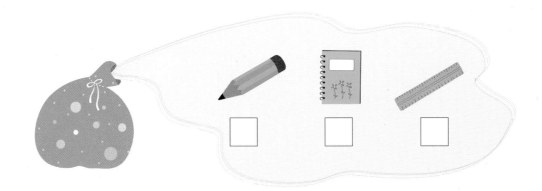

Find the Different Picture and Circle the Word

1

notebook

book

2

pencil case

ruler

Look and Match

bag   pencil
                    ruler
        eraser

book   notebook

Read and Match

1 It's a pencil.

2 It's a notebook.

3 It's a pencil case.

4 It's a ruler.

Look and Match

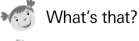 What's that?

It's a bag.

 What's this?

 It's an eraser.

Circle, Match and Trace

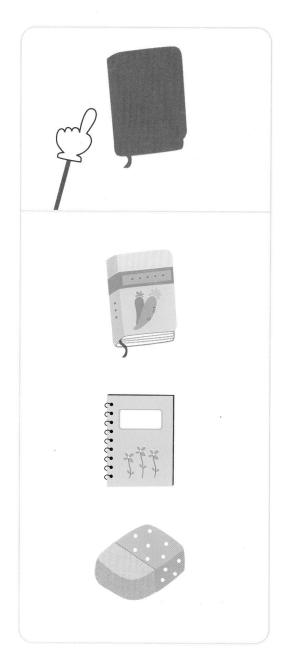

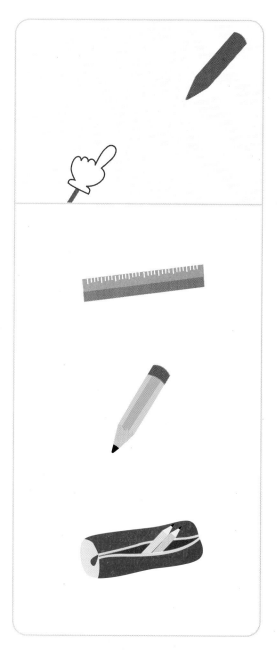

 What's that?

 It's a pencil.

 What's this?

 It's a book.

Listen and Repeat 🎵 T28

| Kk | kid | kite |
| Gg | gorilla | gum |

Listen and Put an X 🎵 T29

ⓐ　　　　ⓑ　　　　ⓒ

Listen and Circle T30

1    k   g

2    k   g

3    k   g

4    k   g

Listen and Write T31

1

[ ] um

2

[ ] orilla

3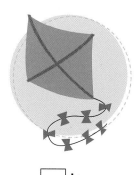

[ ] ite

4

[ ] id

What a Dream!

Read and Number

① It's a pencil. ② What's this?

③ that ④ book ⑤ this

TEST

[1-4] Listen and circle the right picture. T32

1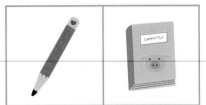

2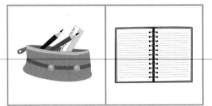

3

4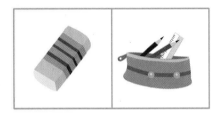

[5-8] Match the word with the right picture.

5 bag •

•

6 notebook •

•

7 pencil case •

•

8 book •

•

[9-12] Listen and choose the right dialog. T33

9

10

11

12

[13-14] Read and choose the right picture.

13
What's this?

It's a ruler.

ⓐ   ⓑ

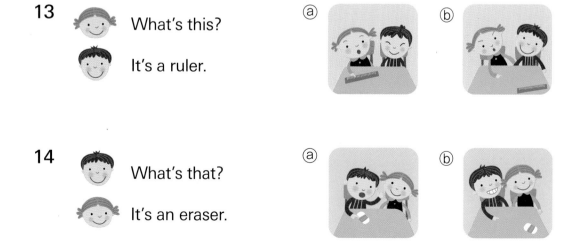

14
What's that?

It's an eraser.

ⓐ   ⓑ

UNIT 04 It's Pink

What color is this?

It's pink.

It's yellow.

🎵 Let's Sing

What color is this? It's pink. It's yellow.
What color is this? It's pink and yellow.

48

Speak Aloud T35

 What color is this?

 It's pink.

1

pink

2

yellow

3
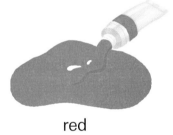
red

4

blue

Listen and Choose T36

ⓐ

ⓑ

ⓒ

Listen and Repeat T37

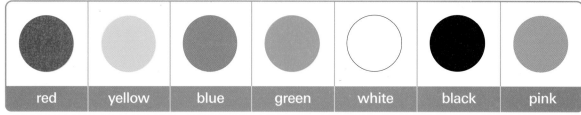

| red | yellow | blue | green | white | black | pink |

Listen and Choose T38

1  ⓐ ⓑ

2 ⓐ ⓑ

50

Look and Circle

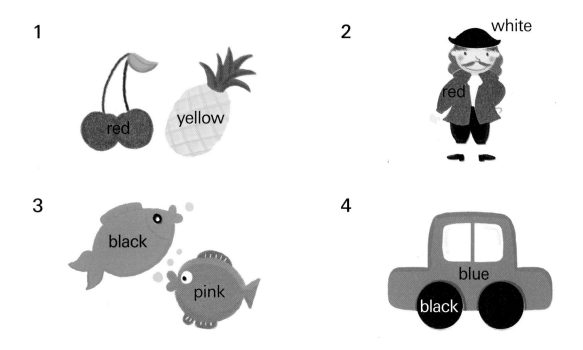

1

red   yellow

2

white

red

3

black

pink

4

blue

black

Find and Match

red

white

green

black

yellow

Put a O or an X

1 **black**   2 **green**

3 **yellow**

Read and Follow

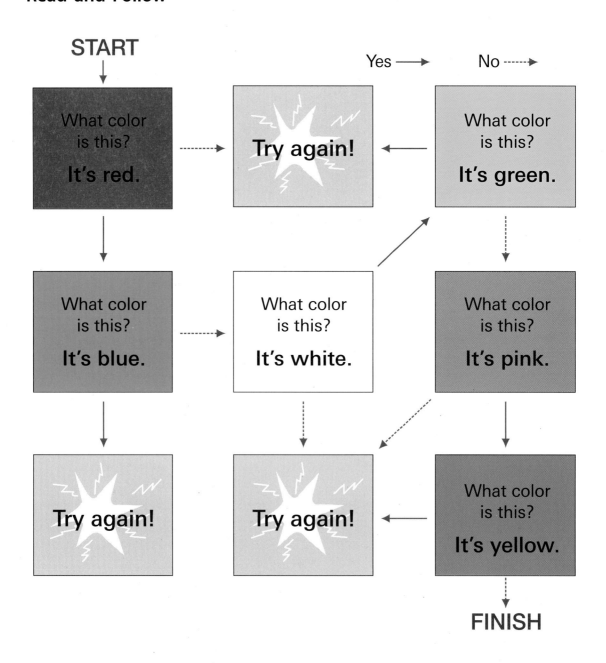

START

Yes ⟶   No ⤑

What color is this?
It's red.

Try again!

What color is this?
It's green.

What color is this?
It's blue.

What color is this?
It's white.

What color is this?
It's pink.

Try again!

Try again!

What color is this?
It's yellow.

FINISH

Follow, Write and Trace

What color is this?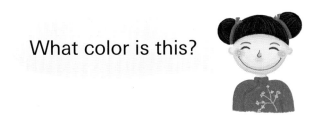

green   pink   red   yellow

1   It's _____ .

2   It's _____ .

3   It's _____ .

4   It's _____ .

5   What color is this?
     It's blue.

Listen and Repeat  T39

Ff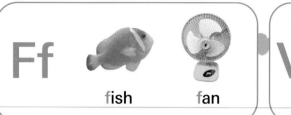

fish   fan

Vv

vase   vet

Listen and Put an X  T40

ⓐ

ⓑ

ⓒ

54

Listen and Match T41

1 f
  v
___et

2 f
  v
___ish

3 f
  v
___an

4 f
  v
___ase

Listen, Match and Write T42

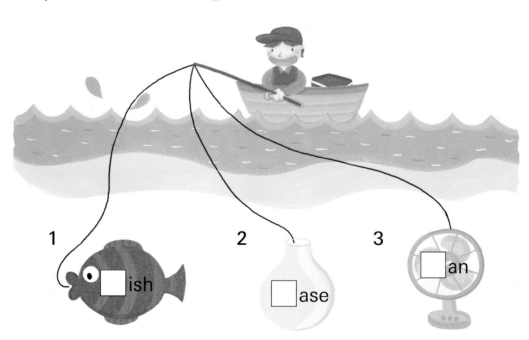

1 ☐ish

2 ☐ase

3 ☐an

f   f   v

A Ghost?

Read and Number

① red　　② vet

③ white　　④ What color is this?

[1-5] Listen and write the number. T43

[6-10] Match the color with the right word.

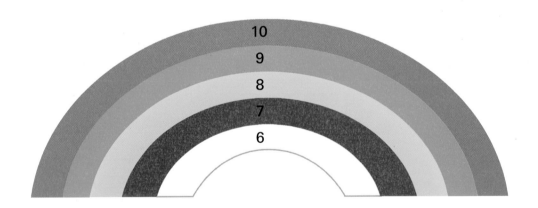

| yellow | white | red | green | blue |

58

[11-13] Listen and choose the correct picture. T44

11 ⓐ   ⓑ

12 ⓐ    ⓑ

13 ⓐ    ⓑ

[14-16] Read the dialog and write the number.

14   *A:* What color is this?
     B: It's green.

15   *A:* What color is this?
     B: It's red.

16   *A:* What color is this?
     B: It's yellow.

Name Bingo

John   Sue   Andy   Kelly
Mary   Tim   Julia   Alex   Justin

준비물 : 연필

❶ 명찰에 보기의 이름을 모두 써 보세요.

❷ 두 명이 짝이 되어 서로 번갈아 가며 한 사람은 What's your name?이라고 묻고, 상대는 이름 하나를 골라 My name is
　　　.라고 대답하세요.

❸ 고른 이름에 두 사람 모두 ×표를 하세요.

❹ 직선 또는 대각선으로 세 줄이 먼저 표시되는 사람이 이기는 게임이에요.

This Or That

준비물 : 주사위, 마커

❶ 각자의 마커를 정하고 주사위를 굴리세요.

❷ 주사위의 눈이 홀수면 1칸, 짝수면 2칸을 이동해 해당 칸 그림을 보고 가까이 있는 사물일 때는 This is a _____.라고
말하고, 멀리 있는 사물일 때는 That is a _____.라고 말하세요.

❸ 맞게 대답하면 이동한 칸에 멈추고, 틀리게 대답하면 예전의 칸으로 되돌아 가세요.

❹ FINISH에 먼저 도착하는 사람이 이기는 게임이에요.

Throw a Coin

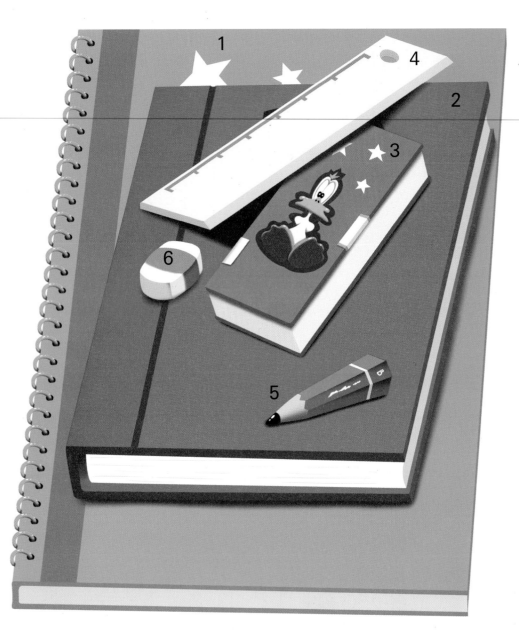

name	score

name	score

준비물 : 동전

❶ 두 명이 한 게임판을 중간에 두고, 게임판 하단 이름 칸(name)에 각자의 이름을 적으세요.

❷ 학생 A가 자리에서 일어나서 동전을 그림 위로 던지세요.

❸ 학생 B가 동전이 놓인 자리의 사물을 가까이에서 가리키면서 What's this? 또는 멀리에서 가리키면서 What's that?이라고 질문하면 학생 B는 It's a(n) _____.라고 대답하세요. 동전이 놓여진 그림에 적혀 있는 숫자만큼 점수를 얻고 점수 칸 (score)에 기록하세요. 동전이 게임판 밖으로 던져졌을 때는 기회를 잃게 되요.

❹ 더 높은 점수를 얻는 사람이 이기는 게임이에요.

What Color Is This?

준비물 : 가위

❶ 두 명이 짝이 되어 각자의 카드를 자른 다음, 카드 두 세트를 섞어 놓으세요.

❷ 두 명이 섞은 카드를 뒤집어서 책상 앞에 펼쳐 놓으세요.

❸ 학생 A가 카드 한 장을 골라 뒤집으면, 학생 B가 What color is this?라고 질문하고, 학생 A는 해당 색을 넣어 It's _____.
라고 대답하세요.

❹ 다시 한 번 ❸의 과정을 반복하세요. 학생 A가 고른 두 장의 카드가 같은 색깔이면 그 카드를 갖고, 다른 색깔이면 다시 뒤집
어 섞고 학생 B에게 기회가 넘어가게 되요.

❺ 더 많은 카드를 가진 사람이 이기는 게임이에요.

Roller Coaster 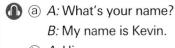 A2
Student Book

UNIT 01

P. 13

🎧 ⓐ *A:* What's your name?
    B: My name is Kevin.
ⓑ *A:* Hi.
    B: Hi.
ⓒ *A:* Bye.
    B: Bye.

ⓐ

P. 14

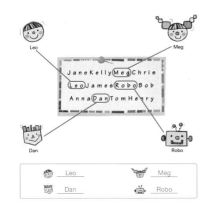

P. 15

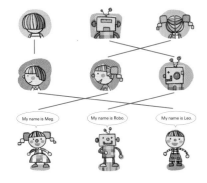

P. 16

1 ◯　　2 ◯　　3 ✕　　4 ◯

P. 17

1 ⓑ　　　　2 ⓒ

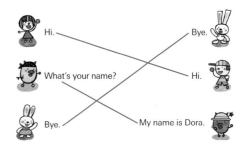

P. 18

🎧 ⓐ bear　　　ⓑ ball　　　ⓒ pear

ⓒ

P. 19

🎧 1 ball　　2 pear　　3 pig　　4 bear

1 | p | b̸ |　　2 | p̸ | b |　　3 | p̸ | b |　　4 | p | b̸ |

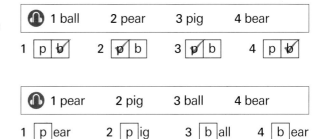

🎧 1 pear　　2 pig　　3 ball　　4 bear

1 | p |ear　　2 | p |ig　　3 | b |all　　4 | b |ear

P. 20-21

CARTOON
② Hi.
My ① name is James.
③ What's your name?

P. 22-23

TEST
[1 - 2]

🎧 1 *A:* Hi.　　*B:* Hi.
   2 *A:* Bye.　*B:* Bye.

1 ⓐ　　　　　2 ⓑ

🎧 3 ⓐ Hi.　　ⓑ Bye.　　ⓒ My name is Meg.

3 ⓒ

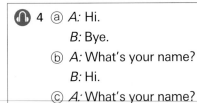 **4** ⓐ *A:* Hi.

B: Bye.

ⓑ *A:* What's your name?

B: Hi.

ⓒ *A:* What's your name?

B: My name is Chris.

4 ⓒ

[5 - 8]

5 ⓐ   **6** ⓑ   **7** ⓒ   **8** ⓑ

UNIT 02

P. 25

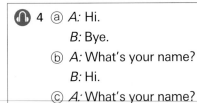 **1** ⓐ This is a desk.

ⓑ That is a desk.

1 ⓐ

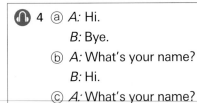 **2** ⓐ This is a blackboard.

ⓑ That is a blackboard.

2 ⓑ

P. 26

window

ⓑ

P. 27

1 door

(chair)

2 desk

(window)

3 (wall)

desk

4 (door)

wall

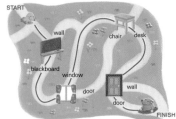

P. 28

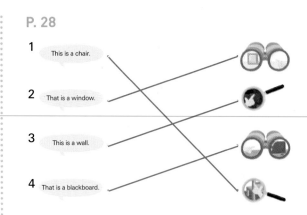

1 This is a chair.

2 That is a window.

3 This is a wall.

4 That is a blackboard.

P. 29

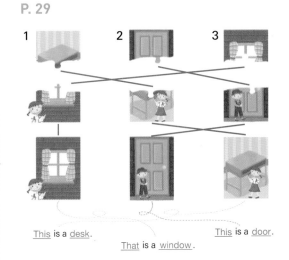

This is a desk.   This is a door.

That is a window.

P. 30

ⓐ dog   ⓑ doll   ⓒ top

ⓐ   ⓑ   ⓒ

P. 31

1 dog   doll

t   (d)

2 top   tea

(t)   d

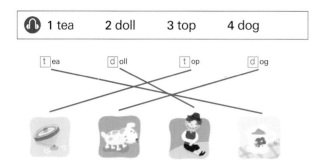

1 tea   **2** doll   **3** top   **4** dog

P. 32-33

CARTOON

This is a ② chair . / That is a ① desk .
③ This is a wall. / ④ This is a door.

P. 34-35

TEST

[1 - 4]

1 door   **2** desk   **3** blackboard   **4** window

[5 - 8]

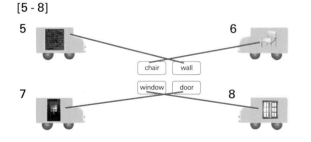

[9 - 11]

9 That is a window.

9 ⓑ

10 This is a desk.

10 ⓑ

11 This is a door.

11 ⓐ

[12 - 14]

12 ②   13 ③   14 ①

UNIT 03

P. 37

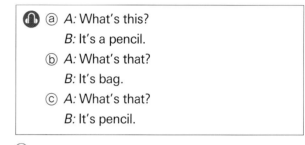

ⓐ *A:* What's this?
    B: It's a pencil.
ⓑ *A:* What's that?
    B: It's bag.
ⓒ *A:* What's that?
    B: It's pencil.

ⓒ

P. 38

1 notebook   **2** pencil   **3** ruler

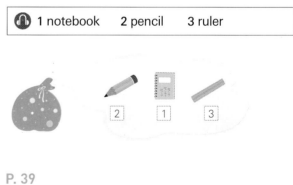

P. 39

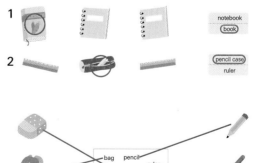
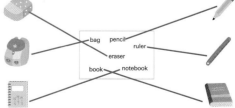

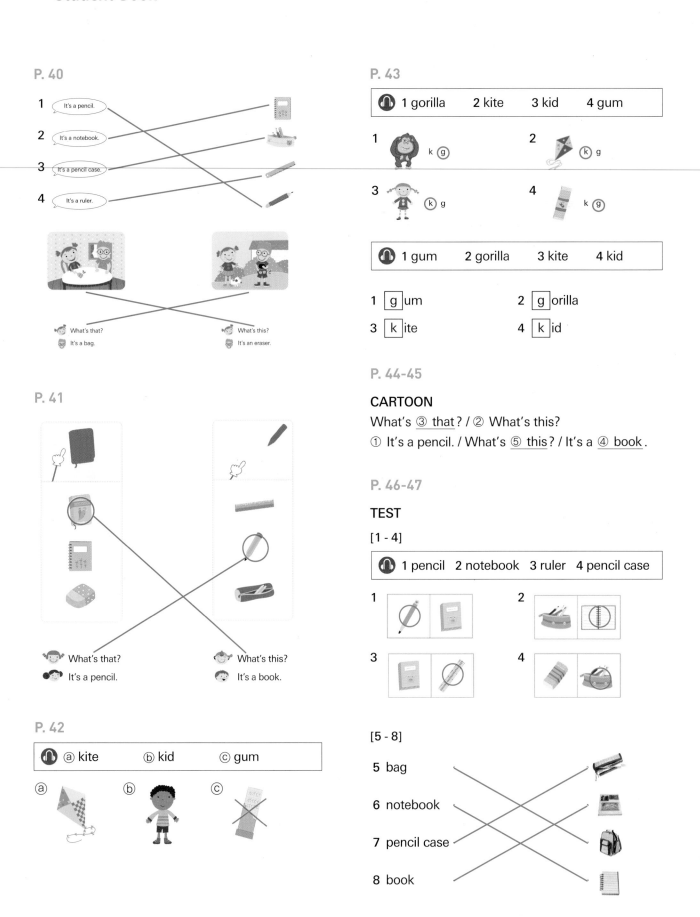

P. 40

1 It's a pencil.
2 It's a notebook.
3 It's a pencil case.
4 It's a ruler.

What's that?
It's a bag.

What's this?
It's an eraser.

P. 41

What's that?
It's a pencil.

What's this?
It's a book.

P. 42

ⓐ kite   ⓑ kid   ⓒ gum

ⓐ   ⓑ   ⓒ

P. 43

1 gorilla   2 kite   3 kid   4 gum

1   k ⓖ   2   ⓚ g
3   ⓚ g   4   k ⓖ

1 gum   2 gorilla   3 kite   4 kid

1 |g| um   2 |g| orilla
3 |k| ite   4 |k| id

P. 44-45

CARTOON

What's ③ that ? / ② What's this?
① It's a pencil. / What's ⑤ this ? / It's a ④ book .

P. 46-47

TEST

[1 - 4]

1 pencil   2 notebook   3 ruler   4 pencil case

1   2
3   4

[5 - 8]

5 bag
6 notebook
7 pencil case
8 book

[9 - 12]

🎧 9 ⓐ A: What's this?
   B: It's a book.
   ⓑ A: What's this?
   B: It's bag.

9 ⓐ

🎧 10 ⓐ A: What's this?
   B: It's a ruler.
   ⓑ A: What's that?
   B: It's ruler.

10 ⓑ

🎧 11 ⓐ A: What's that?
   B: It's a pencil case.
   ⓑ A: What's that?
   B: It's bag.

11 ⓑ

🎧 12 ⓐ A: What's this?
   B: It's an eraser.
   ⓑ A: What's that?
   B: It's an eraser.

12 ⓐ

[13 - 14]
13 ⓐ   14 ⓑ

UNIT 04

P. 49

🎧 A: What color is this?
   B: It's yellow.

ⓑ

P. 50

🎧 1 ⓐ red   ⓑ black

1 ⓐ

🎧 2 ⓐ yellow   ⓑ white

2 ⓑ

P. 51

1   2

3   4

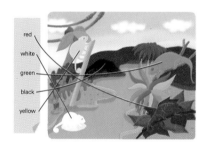

P. 52

1 blck   2 gren   3 yeow

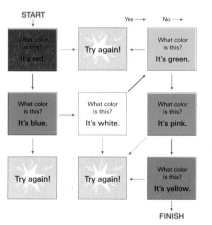

P. 53

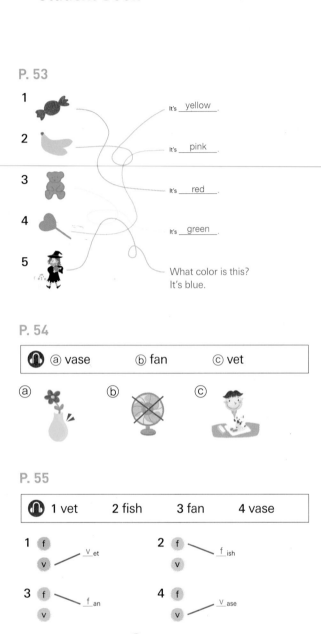

1 It's ___yellow___.

2 It's ___pink___.

3 It's ___red___.

4 It's ___green___.

5 What color is this?
It's blue.

P. 54

| 🎧 ⓐ vase | ⓑ fan | ⓒ vet |

ⓐ   ⓑ   ⓒ

P. 55

| 🎧 1 vet | 2 fish | 3 fan | 4 vase |

1 f
   v ___V___et

2 f ___f___ish
   v

3 f ___f___an
   v

4 f
   v ___V___ase

1 ___f___ish
2 ___V___ase
3 ___f___an
   f   f   v

P. 56-57

CARTOON

④ What color is this? / It's ① red and yellow.

It's ③ white! / He is a ② vet.

P. 58-59

TEST

[1 - 5]

| 🎧 1 green 2 yellow 3 pink 4 red 5 black |

[6 - 10]

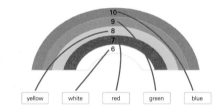

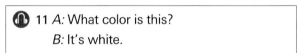

[11 - 13]

| 🎧 11 A: What color is this?
B: It's white. |

11 ⓐ

| 🎧 12 A: What color is this?
B: It's black. |

12 ⓑ

| 🎧 13 A: What color is this?
B: It's blue. |

13 ⓑ

[14 - 16]

14 ③   15 ①   16 ②

Roller Coaster A2
Workbook & Test

UNIT 01

P. 2

B 1 name   2 what   3 pear
   4 pig   5 bear   6 ball

UNIT 02

P. 6

B 1 cl(desk)t   desk
   2 (door)wzo   door
   3 pe(window)   window
   4 ato(wall)q   wall
   5 op(chair)e   chair
   6 (blackboard)er   blackboard

UNIT 03

P. 10

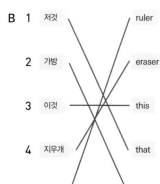

B 1 저것 ─ ruler   ruler
   2 가방 ─ eraser   eraser
   3 이것 ─ this   this
   4 지우개 ─ that   that
   5 자 ─ bag   bag
   6 연필 ─ book   book
   7 책 ─ pencil   pencil
   8 공책 ─ pencil case   pencil case
   9 필통 ─ notebook   notebook

UNIT 04

P. 14

B

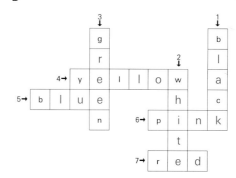

1 검정색의   black
2 흰색의   white
3 초록색의   green
4 노란색의   yellow
5 파란색의   blue
6 분홍색의   pink
7 빨간색의   red

Achievement Test

[1 - 2]

🎧 1 desk
    2 blackboard

1 ✓ T   2 ✓ F

[3 - 5]

🎧 3 My name is Kevin.

3 ⓒ

4 This is a chair.

4 ⓑ

 5 That is a window.

5 ⓐ

6 ⓐ   7 ⓑ   8 ⓐ

9 ⓐ   10 ⓒ

Final Test

[1 - 2]

 1 ruler
   2 yellow

1 ☑ T   2 ☑ F

[3 - 4]

 3 A: What color is this?
   B: It's black.

3 ⓑ

 4 A: What's this?
   B: It's a door.

4 ⓐ

 5 ⓐ It's blue.
   ⓑ It's a desk.
   ⓒ My name is Cindy.

5 ⓒ

6 ⓑ   7 ⓒ   8 ⓑ

9 ⓑ   10 ⓐ

A2

Achievement Test

Name

Score

[1-2] **Listen and check T for true or F for false.** ○ T45

1.

☐ T ☐ F

2.

☐ T ☐ F

[3-5] **Listen and choose the correct picture.** ○ T46

3.
ⓐ  ⓑ  ⓒ

4.
ⓐ  ⓑ  ⓒ

5.
ⓐ  ⓑ  ⓒ

[6-7] **Choose the correct word for the picture.**

6.

ⓐ door
ⓑ wall
ⓒ blackboard

7.

ⓐ desk
ⓑ chair
ⓒ window

8. **Choose the correct sentence for the picture.**

ⓐ This is a wall.
ⓑ That is a wall.
ⓒ This is a window.

[9-10] **Choose the correct sentence for the blank.**

9.

> A: Hi.
> B: _____

ⓐ Hi.
ⓑ Bye.
ⓒ I am Betty.

10.

> A: _____
> B: My name is Eric.

ⓐ Bye.
ⓑ That is my brother.
ⓒ What's your name?

A2

Final Test

Name

Score

[1-2] **Listen and check T for true or F for false.** T47

1.

☐ T ☐ F

2.

☐ T ☐ F

[3-4] **Listen and choose the correct picture.** T48

3.
ⓐ  ⓑ  ⓒ

4.
ⓐ  ⓑ  ⓒ

5. **Listen and choose the correct answer.** T49

> A: What's your name?
>
> B: _____

ⓐ ⓑ ⓒ

[6-8] Choose the correct sentence for the picture.

6.

ⓐ It's white.

ⓑ It's pink.

ⓒ It's blue.

7.

ⓐ This is a book.

ⓑ That is a notebook.

ⓒ This is a pencil case.

8.

ⓐ This is a door.

ⓑ That is a door.

ⓒ This is a window.

9. **Choose the correct sentence for the blank.**

> A: _____
>
> B: My name is Sue.

ⓐ What's this?　　ⓑ What's your name?　　ⓒ What color is this?

10. **Read and choose the correct picture.**

> A: What's this?
>
> B: It's a bag.
>
> A: What color is the bag?
>
> B: It's blue.
>
> A: Good job!

ⓐ

ⓑ

ⓒ

Roller Coaster

WORKBOOK

A Successful Start to Study English

Roller Coaster is a six-level series for elementary school students who are learning English as a foreign language. This series teaches all four language skills: listening, speaking, reading, and writing. Students experience the language in a meaningful way through dialogs, songs, chants, games, and a variety of activities.

A2

01 My Name Is Leo

A Write and say aloud.

1 안녕
(만날 때 인사)
hi

2 안녕
(헤어질 때 인사)
bye

3 무엇
what

4 너의
your

5 나의
my

6 이름
name

7 곰
bear

8 공
ball

9 배
pear

10 돼지
pig

1

B Unscramble the word.

1 e n a m

이름 _____

2 h w a t

무엇 _____

3 p a e r

배 _____

4 p g i

돼지 _____

5 e a b r

곰 _____

6 a l b l

공 _____

C Write and say aloud.

1 너의 이름은 무엇이니?

What's your name?

2 내 이름은 Leo야.

My name is Leo.

3 내 이름은 Meg야.

My name is Meg.

4 내 이름은 Robo야.

My name is Robo.

5 내 이름은 Dan이야.

My name is Dan.

6 너의 이름은 무엇이니?

What's your name?

7 내 이름은 Tom이야.

My name is Tom.

8 내 이름은 Jenny야.

My name is Jenny.

9 내 이름은 Ann이야.

My name is Ann.

10 내 이름은 _____야. (자신의 이름을 쓰세요.)

My name is

02 This Is a Chair

A Write and say aloud.

1 이것   this

2 저것   that

3 칠판   blackboard

4 의자   chair

5 책상   desk

6 문   door

7 벽   wall

8 창문   window

9 앉다   sit

B Find, circle and write the word.

1 c l d e s k t

책상 _____

2 d o o r w z o

문 _____

3 p e w i n d o w

창문 _____

4 a t o w a l l q

벽 _____

5 o p c h a i r e

의자 _____

6 b l a c k b o a r d e r

칠판 _____

C Write and say aloud.

1 이것은 창문이야.

This is a window.

2 저것은 문이야.

That is a door.

3 이것은 벽이야.

This is a wall.

4 저것은 의자야.

That is a chair.

5 이것은 칠판이야.

This is a blackboard.

6 저것은 책상이야.

That is a desk.

7 이것은 문이야.

This is a door.

8 저것은 창문이야.

That is a window.

9 이것은 의자야.

This is a chair.

10 저것은 칠판이야.

That is a blackboard.

03 What's This?

A Write and say aloud.

1 책   book

2 가방   bag

3 공책   notebook

4 자   ruler

5 연필   pencil

6 지우개   eraser

7 필통   pencil case

8 이것   this

9 저것   that

10 무엇   what

B Match and write.

1 저것   ruler   _____

2 가방   eraser   _____

3 이것   this   _____

4 지우개   that   _____

5 자   bag   _____

6 연필   book   _____

7 책   pencil   _____

8 공책   pencil case _____

9 필통   notebook   _____

Write and say aloud.

1 이것은 무엇이니?

What's this?

2 가방이야.

It's a bag.

3 공책이야.

It's a notebook.

4 지우개야.

It's an eraser.

5 연필이야.

It's a pencil.

6   저것은 무엇이니?

What's that?

7   책이야.

It's a book.

8   필통이야.

It's a pencil case.

9   자야.

It's a ruler.

10   지우개야.

It's an eraser.

04 It's Pink

A Write and say aloud.

1　색깔　　　color

2　분홍색의　　　pink

3　빨간색의　　　red

4　파란색의　　　blue

5　노란색의　　　yellow

6　흰색의　　　white

7　검은색의　　　black

8　녹색의　　　green

9　무엇　　　what

B Finish the puzzle.

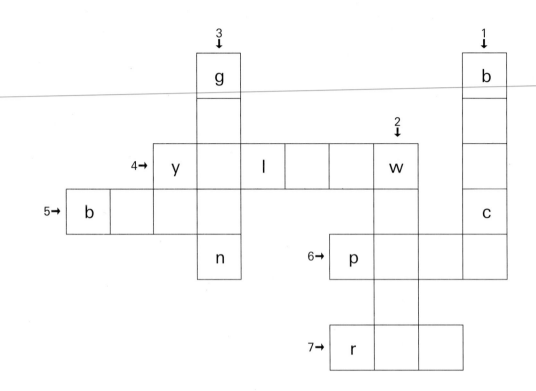

1 검정색의 _____

2 흰색의 _____

3 초록색의 _____

4 노란색의 _____

5 파란색의 _____

6 분홍색의 _____

7 빨간색의 _____

Write and say aloud.

1 이것은 무슨 색이니?

What color is this?

2 분홍색이야.

It's pink.

3 파란색이야.

It's blue.

4 빨간색이야.

It's red.

5 이것은 무슨 색이니?

What color is this?

6 검정색이야.

It's black.

7 흰색이야.

It's white.

8 녹색이야.

It's green.

9 노란색이야.

It's yellow.

Roller Coaster

A Successful Start to Study English